THE POEMS OF EMILY DICKINSON

THE   MS OF M Y   KIN

 (15)

overtakeless (78)

THE MS OF MY KIN

JANET HOLMES

SHEARSMAN BOOKS
EXETER

First published in the United Kingdom in 2009 by
Shearsman Books
58 Velwell Road
Exeter EX4 4LD

http://www.shearsman.com/

ISBN 978-1-84861-035-4

Many thanks to the editors of the following journals for publish-
ing some of the poems herein, occasionally in different form: *1913,
Cannibal, Coconut, Cultural Society, Cutbank, Gutcult, Jumps, Mel-
ancholia's Tremulous Dreadlocks, MiPoesias, Notre Dame Review,* and
Practice: New Literature + Art.

Gratitude also to the following institutions: Boise State University
(for a sabbatical leave), The Foundation Ledig-Rohwolt and the
Chateau de Lavigny, The Idaho Commission on the Arts, and The
National Endowment for the Arts (US).

Cover design by Quemadura.

These poems are erased from Emily Dickinson's poems of 1861 and 1862, the first years of the United States Civil War. Each poem of mine is titled by the year in which Dickinson composed the original(s), its order in the current sequence, and (in parentheses) the Franklin numbers of the erased poems. I owe the project to the invitation of its epigraph.

If it had no pencil,
Would it try mine —

E.D., #184

AGAIN, FOR AL

_J_

at
Sunrise —   a Flag

How short it takes to make

                Victory

                        hear them
        bustle

fumble at   Prayer —

        coming
                    before

The   Country

Martyrs —
Their

Company —

Streaks
Opon a Planet's

Air —

then

two
come

No
No

Dawn

means   Risk —
Revelation —

Apocalypse —

Anguish

again —

1861.3 (192–199)

Transport

clad in

a trick

Does'nt —   move —

without
                    me —

God gives us

Victory —

lips

take it —

so economical

little mouths

know how to starve —

Confronting
      the Adamant

Mind

          near his nest

        how late — how late —

Transporting

the fire   burn

the Centuries

men

fumbled

Till those two troubled

the Desert
With

a fine invention

Emergency

more distinctly seen —
                    the surge

reached the other side —

Come slowly

Round

Least   docile

Yield

Reeling —

        renounce

          the

           hunt —

lost   World —

Give
A Memorial   —

        no
Granite   !

    an Organ

            no word —
        breath

            what was done to me

        one cannot
transport

        Ghosts in Cages

What sorcery

would not

do,

they

Did

Heart!

Heart —

when Time is over —

will   each separate

           tell
                            his woe
              the

              long
              late morn
                                Elephants

                   rose   their
           gales
                              the eyes
                              shone

           quiet   of death —

       A Witch   yieldeth

                       to

                   my will
       If anybody
             care

1861.7 (217–223)

You

cheated
grinning

night will   be
home to

a little dull
pain

welcome

I
spotted

a little thing —

yet

I was strong

He was strong

Neither — was strongest —

somebody bring the light
So

Death wont hurt —

light —
setting sun

1861.8 (224–228)

awful

creatures

shook their fists —

finished that

Girl's life

Stop there!

plea —

Oh God!

Her

        Heart —

I hear the

    transport

           — in brass and scarlet —

It is

               Men
          service in the place

Where

    Wilderness — can be

    Desert Noon —

we hide our brave

dream

to the end —

Take us   Lord —

He   — and I   remembered

                                fire

A Slash

                        between

                                eyes
That hunted —

                        it broke
    useless as   morning's

blame

going
Home

Some
wear   Wings —
instead

the Heart

sent

To climb

at your side

                                                        staggered —

             Try —
             Try —

                                        dream

                     it's

                     play

the fall of

Who live there —

they know

the soul   in pain —

simple,

Like a Panther

                                          dropped

Into
        a Face
    suddenly

                    Death
            drills his Welcome in

            "Found dead" —

the Setting Sun

supremer —

✓ *spangled*   —

A C .

The

One!

It matters

             that the oil
                  is gone.

One life

        would pay —

      Pearl —
That

      cost

     burns

The
    Bad men

        offended

    his

    Empire

    intercede

If   *nothing — more*
—

God —

the pulse *just*

quivering —
"consider"

that
Some   were moved

By   *trust* —

1861.15 (253–255)

These
          fetching Stars

                    puzzle us

          the

Company

                    shift s
          tone

                    to fear —

wrestles

Forgets

all

Cuckoo

rules   —

Britain

discerns

a
shining

Retreat —
America —

No Trace   of the Thing
That dazzled

Men, and Feats

swallowed up

like   Blood

the puppet
just now

quivered out   —

It

— concernless   —

Nods

Decades of Arrogance

Nobody

admiring

The day

                    gone —
        now   remembrance

You are
                no one

Or

                    very far

                                    from me —

                    time for me

to walk

away
beloved Heart —

we can never learn
Change —

It cant be
    got through!

   that long town of

    "Dying"

   shall go in

  Cuffs

        see his face?

  that is not

     let

You know who

        "shares"

Dominions—

Now

        pay
                this

        Contract

          's worth

Rearrange a
                Brain!
Amputate
               a man!

      spirit, in thy
      unacknowledged

Constancy

None suspect

it's *bandaged* —
will never get away

see   them
            shut the door!

Oh,   the Gentleman
In   "White Robe" —

               forbid?

Wild

Wild

        Heart
Done with

            singing

Late —

Over the fence

would

climb —

Captive!

ashamed of that

Dishonor

bend   low

Again —   voice   at the door

to *justify*
He never *saw*   *this*

The *other's*

Dog

Goes

First

        to

The   *Vein* —

    doomed

       to die

            unheard —

Civilization

      never rebuked her

She was

     the
      keeper —

Pity   left her

Going to
Tell
Tell
Tell

they

You
Tell

           were silenter

begged to be ended —

That day

      the Souls that
      Elected

    Subterfuge

                carved away
Behold

The World

    bears another's — name —
      if it be fair

The Man —   the Woman —

or a lesser

superior

qualified for

our new
        Tactics

should have been

                blamed —

should have had
the Fear

to understand

The Zeros
        learned to like

                        power

That
        smites
And

                appalls

        suggests

        the

Whip

Until Death touches
it

chanting "Live"!

She tied the Hoods to

every shoulder

to hide

Who

affronts

The   men

Elephant
Look further   .

others — show

Like Juggler's Figures

It   halts —

Denying   it was —

got so
            Tremendous
That Stop-sensation
And Thunder —

            that forcing,

        to   Extremity —

Petition's
        ignorant

        Business —
        Power
Not subject to

            ✓

        the Soul

                    put away
                              as if no plight
          Had

              just turned

          Into Eternity —

                         the Peril's

              greater than
          They

          Will   it   —

A Weight

this

Heart
had not strength to hold —

Fantastic

Mystery!

Night after Night

men
vanish   !

The Doomed
With   Delight —

The Man — to die — tomorrow —

Joyful —

Joyful —

Just one
Charge

                    men
                                who prefer   the Glory
And their

        God's

                martial

                            march

1862.6 (300—305)

farther Parted, than

Twelve months ago —
We

the patientest

53

— how soon?

It's

Everlasting

They have no

Home

Coming

they're never   —

Heaven

Lift
        the Boy —

Homesick   steadfast   —
Ah —

                Escaped —

1862.7 (305–306)

They cannot take

        Guns

As

        a Travelling Show
   who died   yesterday

       for

       souls — away —

Who is to blame?

God should

                      drop a life

Into
    plummetless

             bliss

     then —

         softly —

       stirless —

Kill

reach

"Heaven" —   !

The
      interdicted Land —

            Paradise —

            spurned us —

Kerouac

(152)

(On) 1862.9 (311—312)
off the Road

two
hand the Tools

by night
a
gag —

None

see who's there

A Watch

sleeping —

Screams

And Echoes —

just

Pools of

Pain

How many
How many

"Hope" is the

tune without the

Bird

the chillest
strangest

sunshine

That once
Blazed

in my   gazing — face —

now —   it

Turns   away

that flight

Struck

Lives —

leaves the shreds behind—
Oh
Come back —

You
You

Her

So distant —

Universe,

vaster
And

Completeless ✓

There's a certain

       Heft

Shadows — hold
       like
     Death

       quenching
        the Sky

        's

        Candle

     — for You

the Dark

might have been

the Camp —

Men

And   Women

Passed

Into

the Desert

a Day

no Soul

Was

Permitted to

look

at   the Grave

lonesome for

the old Mountains

Scarlet

lip

the odd

Kennel —

Just
Solitude —

They

who overcame

"Defeat"

stood — whispering

the Flesh
            wants
        more —

snap

Life
Deliberate, as   up —
Kingdoms

do

He had no

conversation —

was

appalling

Dim

the Life —

the Woman

ceded all of

Heaven,

laughter

like
the Tide's

weep

for the Sorrow, done me —
Joy

despatched abroad

the Boughs

Beyond
Beyond

Hid

Birds

        Grace   —
     Outcast   —

parted Rank —

hurt
herself,
a Ball she got —
And

happy   sudden —

smiling —
Just consummated —
this one, wears
pain
Fresh

I got my eye put out —

(155)

                    my Heart
        split,

The Meadows —
The Mountains —
All Forests —

            finite

The Motions of
    Morning's

        news   strike me dead —

1862.18 (336–342)

The

                              Oddity —

            we buried

            the Jacket   he
            buttoned in the
                        mornings,

The

Tie

The Beads

                strung

   Service

           Boots

         an Ear,

Wrecked,

And
And
And
And

so appalling

To know the worst

The Truth,

If
We

Stop

Just let

Others   wrestle

Terror's

O'ertakeless   A.C.

Sweep

1862.19 (342–347)

we stand

The smoke
And mirrorrs   the

                                    wink
              the flaw —
The

                              Head
Where others,   not
Protected

              wanted to get out
       some

              would

blur the

        grieved
     thought
How   some
      should come to

Death —

comprehend

       ?
   trust the
           head?
  impeach

And   brake

Him

D
  own

1862.20 (347–349)

So foreign   —

He

could not bear   ,
wished they'd

stayed away

            acknowledge
    their unthinking

                    picture —

It's   impossibility

        sweet

            talk, like
            the
Raised
            easy

            Balloon

awful

to

                    live to know
such a day

1862.21 (349–353)

silenced,

I'm different

My
      face

                  will
                 turn   to

one long

                look of

                    hungry

   Hope

the Infinite

shall

trust

                                    me

        — I've stopped being Their's —

Called to
Existence

    half   conscious   —
But
With Will

such and such

in the Sepulchre —

on such a
date —

You try to

tell

the Company

That dont remember

It was not

It was
their

was not   Flesh

just

Figures

        fitted to a frame
        could not breathe

                    ticked
And

        the Beating

                    — Stopless —
Without a Chance

I could see

        fear

           when his life was out —

uncertain

if it was there —

the Owner

pushed   and waited —

Conviction

too

.

easy

did not know I saw —

He

     looked   frightened

Like one in danger

The   Bandaged

   feel   Fright
And

    freezing   —

             escape

       a Bomb

Long Dungeoned

           the news of

their

bright

Lives

Spare

d

keep

our

Heart

almost
Content

1862.24 (363–367)

he
practised

Recording

soft Refrains

of Adamant

to
numb

our
Children to

dumb the
Revelations

He
— in silence —
hid

to make

Death's   stare —

Look
        not
                too

                strong   —

But   he

                failed!

        for what wrong
did

their

      Head
s fall

     they held —

   they bore

He
Spoke of
That   journey —

Heaven —

    wealth   —
  ⸗ happy — happy "'   —

    just abroad

                    boldly
    tell Him   No —
                No —
    interdict —

            fictitious

                the
        everlasting
                        perfect
            Delight

        Blesseder
            then
To

        save
                another

a   feeling

Yesterday

Of Ground

                                        letting go

—

1862.27 (373–375)

This World

baffles —

Men
of

Faith slip   — and
                see
                        Evidence —

                in
        lies —

their

Reward for   this —

Empire

1862.28 (376–377)

the old — road —
unfrequented —

she passed —

swift —

Look!
turn   back

Herself —   fled!

Another bed
make

out of sight —
For
her Head!

in
which   chamber is

the
Maelstrom

?

who heard
    the Birds

knew

No one could
        perfect
      that

                  Eden —

          surrender
the

    legend
and the
      telling

When the last
        silence
      strikes

Sphere of

too common

perishing —

dream

the letters I can write

were

dance

Or

—like Birds —

sound,

mention
    me

coming Home

to stay

I

have a way —

a Pile of Mountains —

crawl between

chase

Then
Stop —

It don't sound so terrible   as it did —
I

Shift
            To

new Things —

It's shrewd

        the

Next — One —
Could

                              mend my old One —

And   mine —
       the joy of feeling

       high —

       when I die

          — how rich I go —
        impeach
And banish me —

1862.32 (386–390)

the fair Ideal,

we discover

a lie —

We adored

Him —

Obedient to

command

It would never be

that   sort

now

As

all the World

suddenly   shrank

back

They   remember
the

People

of Death —

how to forget

they

died
In
Sacrifice

But

to

an

invention

Of

cool
Disposers —

we

occupy

another

One

not

meant

For

us

again —

The   last

        hand
                was my
                                        Raise

        He

        took   —
                    paid
The   price,

            handed me
A single

            broke forth
And
                        ran

he thought
men

did not Care

here
They'd modify

Judgment

— Surrender   — Cancel

And leave   alone —

I think

It suits

That men

in the Desert

thrive   on

The Gnash of

play,

And

Dare

the Fire's
vivid

conditions —

it's

soundless

Refining

Blaze

To hear   sing
    a common

Crowd

"No Sir!   "

        is
   Anguish

But

      we could die —
The best

  reason

To put this   down
And walk   away

his   Confederates

                              sowed

Clusters

every drop

      put away   life

       low as mine
might have been

    sowed

               pain,
Or
Or

      the least
   just
         delighted it

A
   "Hide and Seek"—
Or
Or   chase   —

The Surgeon will not
            will have   to
        will

        will

        may

Over and over

the

Haunted

Brain

meeting

it

self   —

in
Horror   —

borrows a Revolver

More

Old fashioned

Tradition

1862.38 (409-410)

Society —

Unmoved —   notes

an ample nation

in

pain —

And   turned

1862.39 (411)

Mine —   the   Election!
Mine
Mine

Mine
Mine

Mine —   A   steal!

//

She   at

Arms,
As if for   sport —

Her   Eyes

   sparkling

Devising   a
   force
               so deep

            it
Could not   be proved

         our idea

To Him

    'tis

        solemn!

       the   Press

    Imagery

      Parades —

Flags,   a brave sight —

      triumphant —

               He went

Lit with

A Power

      just adequate

    — an Ampler Zero —

Citizen

Who
Ignores the   News

The   ends

        of

                              lives

                    put away —

By

              His

          power

1862.42 (418–421)

Riches —

Dominions —

the Commonest

Wealth

Without a stint —

each Day,

solaces

I prove
It's

simple

124

Death is   Common

      privilege

                is large

        a   Thing
So
Naked

Which

                  Forces

That
   far

           trouble
              back—

     altered,

I

                nestled Close

To Cushions

'twas
Peace —

1862.43 (422–423)

Give little
Lives

    they'll

  make no

           Speech

       a thing

      to atoms blown —

  another
     Day

       my face

     begun to laugh —

And
My Brain keeps giggling —

  Something's odd —

Could it be Madness

1862.44 (424)

Grave
Grave

help

Grave
Grave

Grave

You've seen

it   before

the Agony

Toyed coolly with

you

Until you felt your

Sense   numb —

your

                    Doubt

                the utterest —

I gave Myself to

The solemn

           Vision

         in the
   subtle   lie —

Some

         predicted
          them
   do   us
           wrong

We

    witness

A Moment

     fit our Vision to the Dark

And meet the

larger — Darkness

The Bravest
                    hit
Directly

                              know 'tis
    Glory —

    Glory

                    and

            Might
Assert themselves —

1862.47 (429–431)

The Lady   ʻ

     peers beyond her mesh —

     contented —

Think of it Lover!
       face to face
           we'll say

How Midnight felt
How all the Clocks stopped   the World
              'Twas so cold

We look back
At those Old Times

to look at

Paradise

1862.48 (432)

my sentence

extremest

                              shame —

"God have mercy" on the Soul

at the last,

Salute, and pass,
        there, the Matter Ends —

1862.49 (433–434)

in the Trees

find

A long — long Yellow

Our

Hurrying Home
To
All

Of

them

I promised ne'er to
break My word

No fear

It is dead —
Out of Sight —
Which is wiser —
You, or the

low Ground?

in this World

    this   is said to be

        rare —
        to

      choose

     some one else
And leave
Himself

                   in the Dark —

Home
like Paradise

never comes

they say

Myself would run

to
It's

secure — inviting —

shelter

I had been

trembling

hungry,

could not hope

did not know

felt ill — and odd —
                                    Bush

                            found
                    a way
Of
        entering

My   Life

I leaned opon the Awe —

                    an Ocean
        broke against my ear —

                fear

                        compassed

                me

You'll find — it
        easier to
        recollect

                their
                        names

        when this

                tawdry

        Love of
        Viole

                                        n
                                c
                e

                be

held

                              for

        Nought

        And   a living child —

                         more
        Than
                    a

                    Gnat

They shut   up

For Treason

Him

          That

                    was not

unconscious

a Man

                they
        know

could be heard

Oh, Reward

                    for Truth

Dreams — are   better

      at

        confronting

      the

      Axis

    — spin

    paints

It's   precise
    Brand

On

The   whole

feared

Destiny

— Home —

Borne on

fit

gain

we

stand up   —

some sovreign

few
Smile — and alter — and prattle —

Our journey
            almost
To that
            Term

        took sudden awe —

    Forest of the Dead —

Retreat — was out

        because
        it would be

power dropped —

I sang firm

I

          must pass
Through

    the Grave —

    Worlds

we

       knew not   till then

They

    did not dare
For fear

                  of

The

   Prison

       to look
For the
    deal   stated as Our

                Posture
        That
                            — Not so real
                    Liberty —

        something passiver —

        Liberty
                like a Dream
                for any

Sometimes

    they do not die —

    who have

        bared
        a Bone —

      Steel's
      grimace in the Flesh —
How

        — not polite —

      to

       require

reasons

Therefore —

Transport
            such
                Tent by Tent
                        Flags

        Cover
Not
                                    Us —

        notice Us — no more —
                            turn away
                    o'er and o'er

The General

— dazzling pace —

makes no show for

An independent   —

Was ever   like

            the

other   s
the Twitter
opposite

        the Whole —

wished a way
to
magnify
the

Blood
opon
the Road —   (59)

far

away —

Possibility —

Superior —

for an everlasting

Occupation —

A Solemn thing
To
            hang
The Maker   —
        the
            Being

You thought was finished —

But
Your   Harvest
            — Every sun
    —   some lives.

1862.60 (468—472)

Gulf
　　　　of solid Blood -
　　　　the

　　　　appointed Creature

bows　　and

　　　　fetches

And
　　could be

　　　　like

The Minor One　　that

　　　　cared to please

　　　　the mighty

(none could see   (15)

1862.61 (472–476)

I was

stationed

—

just
            think
That   was all —

never spoke — unless addressed —

The Racket shamed me   —

had not been
one I knew

— I

cannot see -

further

pretending

To

                                    toil
Against   Man
                          — I

Relate
                    to
              them —

He

stuns you by Degrees —

the   Blow
                    further
Then nearer — Then

your naked soul —

                    in their Paws —

Adamant

    put
agonizing terms

down

    I could not stop

My labor

We passed the
   Recess -

           He passed Us
The   Chill
   on

        the Ground —

Since then — 'tis

Eternity -

He   like those Who've nought to lose
Bestowed   to

Us

Men,

His Comrades

left alive
to die

to justify

This   honorless
futile Diadem —

the
General

Rendered
"Sweet"
Liberty

won   by

possession —
in the land —

Could I

Not opon   knee   thank

And

Praise

the

Benefactor
Making

Blank
A   Way

To   advance

ends
disclosed —

it came
by degrees -

reprieves

long enough for

rallying
—

a

kiss
with

Mother
Or Father —

on the Lawn
Indicative that

Darkness   is about to pass

I deemed

    therefore

That I   adjust

My Faith
  when
My Faith

        steps

    abroad
To do His   Will

How dare I

            fail

The
        Men —

We want
Honors —

Flags —

      a friend's Hand —

      the Ministry   —

To offer brave
   Lives

           Divine

          Benediction

Not a
          cool
Hope
Not

                    lying   —
        Yet   Nature

                 was still —

                 forget
                   that
                    —

        Memory

             did'nt come

                                 Declare —
        Were you   there?

His business
has been

To

fling Sand,

"Get out of the Way, I say"
Who'd
Would you
be the fool to stay?

The Day
of Gold
of Purple
old

as the World
And yet

Too near

Candle
Flickering

in the Cold
Trudging
World —

The Cruel — smiling —   World —
    it's

              forgotten —
The

         Hands
Lifted

   supplicate

One
    be finished

The
   Danger
Is

            — opon the Soul

To go without
   challenging Despair.

People and events referenced in the poems, and occasional speakers of the poems, include those piloting aircraft on 9/11; U.S. President George W. Bush; Osama bin Laden; U.S. Vice President Dick Cheney; U.S. Defense Secretary Donald Rumsfeld; the pro-war Republican Congress (the elephant is the symbol of the Republican Party in the U.S.); soldiers, terrorists, occupiers, insurgents, and combatants on both sides of both the wars in Afghanistan and Iraq; Afghani and Iraqi civilians; *Wall Street Journal* reporter Daniel Pearl; British Prime Minister Tony Blair; prisoners at Abu Ghraib and Guantanamo Bay facilities and their guards; those injured by improvised explosive devices, gunfire, bombs, and other means; Pfc. Lynndie England; Spc. Charles Graner; families of those killed on 9/11; families of U.S. soldiers killed in Iraq and Afghanistan; war resisters both inside and outside the military; Muslim and Christian religious leaders; U.S. Secretary of State Condoleeza Rice; the phenomenon of displaying yellow ribbons to indicate one "has not forgotten" soldiers fighting the war; former Ambassador Joseph C. Wilson, IV; the "Bush Doctrine"; Gen. Peter Pace; and Gen. David Petraeus.

AUTHOR

Janet Holmes is author of *F2F, Humanophone, The Green Tuxedo,* and *The Physicist at the Mall.* She is editor of Ahsahta Press and a professor in the MFA program for creative writers at Boise State University. She lives in Idaho with her husband, the novelist and poet Alvin Greenberg.

3·17·18 c 1:31 am
(TOST 3: 5)

CPSIA information can be obtained at www.ICGtesting.com
Printed in the USA
BVOW030445220213

313913BV00001B/17/P